Patrick Lubjuhn

From Path-Dependency to Knowledge-Based Economy - Analysi
-

GRIN - Verlag für akademische Texte

Der GRIN Verlag mit Sitz in München hat sich seit der Gründung im Jahr 1998 auf die Veröffentlichung akademischer Texte spezialisiert.

Die Verlagswebseite www.grin.com ist für Studenten, Hochschullehrer und andere Akademiker die ideale Plattform, ihre Fachtexte, Studienarbeiten, Abschlussarbeiten oder Dissertationen einem breiten Publikum zu präsentieren.

Patrick Lubjuhn

From Path-Dependency to Knowledge-Based Economy - Analysing the Finnish ICT Miracle -

GRIN Verlag

Bibliografische Information der Deutschen Nationalbibliothek: Die Deutsche Bibliothek
verzeichnet diese Publikation in der Deutschen Nationalbibliografie; detaillierte bibliografische Daten sind im Internet über http://dnb.d-nb.de/ abrufbar.

1. Auflage 2005
Copyright © 2005 GRIN Verlag
http://www.grin.com/
Druck und Bindung: Books on Demand GmbH, Norderstedt Germany
ISBN 978-3-640-66752-9

From Path-Dependency to Knowledge-Based Economy

- Analysing the "Finnish Miracle" -

Twente University
School of Business, Public Administration and Technology
European Economic Policies
Patrick Lubjuhn

10.01.2006

Introduction

Structural change has taken place all over Europe in the last decades. Phenomenons like globalization and internationalization of enterprises and markets have allowed free movement of capital and growing mobility. We are now "on the way to a global economy". Globalization has made it necessary for national economies to accept and implement a sort of transformation process. With globalization, a new kind of competition game has emerged, of course with its own, new rules. Innovation abilities of national countries have become a central aspect in winning this game, or at least to gain some positive outcomes of it. So on the one hand each national economy must make sure to join this game and on the other hand not to fall by the wayside. Furthermore it has to adjust its national clusters and paths´ to innovative and future-oriented developments. Concerning most literature about this topic, its focus lies on central regions and processes like the structural change in the Ruhr Area. For me it is worth to take a look at Europe's most peripheral regions as well since taking a glance beyond one's own nose might reveal success stories and best-practices which could eventually add something to a positive economic and socio-economic development in the EU as a whole and in its member states, respectively.

One of these peripheral areas is Finland. The fact that Finland is far away from the centres of European economic activities, for example the so-called blue banana, the Sunbelt and the Industrial axe, its relative economic success, especially in the field of information and communication technologies (ICT) makes it so interesting to analyse what is so characteristic for the "Finish-ICT Miracle", as Paija (2001) has called it. During the last decade, Finland has become one of the world's most successful technology-intensive countries, finding itself in the front rank of the world's digital economies. In a decade, Finland went from being one of the least information and communication technologies specialized countries to become the single most specialized one. "Currently the Finnish ICT sector, with Nokia as its locomotive, consists of some 6 thousand firms and accounts for approximately 10 percent of Finland's GDP" (Rouvinen & Antilla 2003, p.87) and therefore have put Finland on the map of global economies. Determining for this "raise" of Finland is the development of a new growth path in this small Nordic country. Finland has managed to transform itself from a resource-based into a knowledge-based economy in a rather short period of time, especially without any major cutbacks in his highly developed welfare state system. The essential point of analysis in my essay deals with the question, how Finland managed to

become one of the most successful ICT-countries in the world. How was it possible for this small Nordic country to go through a structural change from forestry to ICT? Nowadays, "about 6000 firms (mostly small and medium-sized) and 200 electronics manufacturing services companies make up the so called 'ICT cluster'. Some 350 of them are first-tier suppliers to Nokia, and represent the 'Nokia network'" (Daveri & Silva 2002, p.9).

So I will start my analysis by defining structural change to create a basic which is necessary to understand the whole process. With the use of statistical data I will then try to explain Finland's way from forestry to ICT. A central aspect of the recent Finnish ICT-cluster is the importance of the mobile telecommunication industry with its driving engine, Nokia. This is analysed in part three. And finally of course, my essay ends up with a conclusion, summing up all the relevant information which is necessary to explain how Finland has turned into a knowledge-based economy.

Concerning methodology it has to be said that my work is based on recent scientific articles and essays instead of books simply because I want to keep it as actual as possible. Also statistical data is used from the internet (www.finfacts.com) and from some OECD-reports, cited in the relevant articles which I have used in my essay.

1)   Defining "Structural Change"

Before I am going to start starting my analysis, it is first useful to define what is actually meant by the term 'structural change', so that we can better understand what has happened, and what actually is going on in Finland's economy . In my point of view, "structural change" describes a more or less constant change of the contribution of the different sectors of the economy to the gross domestic product (GDP). The contribution of some economic sectors, like for example agriculture or forestry, to the aggregate economic product has steadily declined, while at the same time, the share of other branches of the economy, like the service sector in modern times, has grown increasingly. Structural change is accelerated by the development of new technologies as well as the increasing international competition (Pollert, Kirchner & Polzin 2004) and processes like globalization.

Schumpeter supported this briefly described, basic idea of structural change as well. He also considers the development of new technologies, or, as he puts it, "new combinations" (Hospers 2003, p.79) as the essence of structural change, because they

lead to a process of "creative destruction through which the old economic structure is destroyed and a new one is created". This "creative destruction" process described by Schumpeter is an important act to consider in my following work as well.

According to Hospers (2003, p. 81) the French economist and "father of the structural change theory", Jean Fourastié, goes one step further than Schumpeter and does not only see innovations as the driving force behind structural change: He claims that structural change, in the first place, can be explained through the "imbalance between the growth of production and consumption". This means that because of consumers demanding more and more services while at the same time the growth of production taking place in the first and second sector the economy has to go through a structural change in order to be able to handle this supply/demand bias.

In a knowledge-based economy, firms are dependent on the knowledge resources of other firms. Especially in the information and communication technology (ICT) industry, technological race and shortening product life cycles have forced companies to focus on their core-competencies and to get access to the resources of other specialised companies. This is done by inter-firm contracts or networking. Fruitful inter-firm activities induce knowledge spillovers and accumulation as well as technology transfers, which in turn stimulate innovations. According to Paija (2000, p.2), "increased outsourcing of equipment manufacturers (OEM) and deepening partnerships with subcontractors has marked the organisational development in the industry in the 1990s". In Finland, to be concrete, Nokia in particular has created very confidential relations with its key partners, who enable early development of future products, and which is a precondition for the technological leadership Nokia pursues.

Now I will try, having the thoughts about "structural change" in mind, to turn to the development in Finland in detail, by analysing whether this structural change, together with a possible path-shift, took place or not.

2) Structural Development in Finland

2.1) Historical Backdrop

-The Phase of Path-Dependency –

Of course, Finland's transition to a high-tech economy has not really taken place as suddenly as it seems. In the background is a long, self-strengthening and complex development process that started early in institutions, organisations and throughout the Finnish society with the beginning of the 1900s. The dominance of the ICT-cluster in Finland in the time under Russian rule especially was relevant for the discussion. Looking back to the middle of the 19th century, in contrast to other European countries, Finland was still highly underdeveloped and far away from industrialization. The majority of the Finns lived in rural areas, which were dominated by self-sufficient economy. At that time, "only some 30,000 Finns worked in industry. That is about half of the workforce of Nokia"[1] today. In my point of view the main reason for this underdevelopment up to the mid 1800s was Finland being poor of natural resources. Except for some copper, the only relevant income source of the Finnish economy has been timber for a long time. This relevance became even more significant when other European states started demanding more wood than they could supply themselves. Because of this increasing demand for wood, especially as a material for railroads, construction, mining, and paper, Finland could finally start its industrialization. Therefore it can be followed that the decisive factor for the Finnish take-off phase was the endowment of its most important and virtually only natural resources: forests.

Quick advancement in prosperity towards the end of the 1800s and in the early 20th century was based on rapidly growing exports of forest-related products—first timber and later, pulp and paper. From the late 1950s to the late 1970s, the Finnish forest industry carried out massive investments and transformed itself gradually into a global technology leader most modern and efficient production capacity in the world According to Rouvinen & Anttila (2003, p.9), "by the late 1980s, the forest sector had developed into a competitive industrial cluster that today provides high value-added paper grades, as well as forestry technologies and consulting services". One the one hand it can be followed that Finland was characterised by a path-dependency of the

---

[1] http://www.finnfacts.com/english/country/story/theroad/industrialization.html

forestry but that on the other hand, this path-dependency had made Finland growing and made it competitive.

Figure 1:

Figure 1. **The Fastest Growing European Country in the Postwar Era:**
GDP Volume in Finland and OECD-Europe (in 1995 prices and purchasing power parity exchange rates)

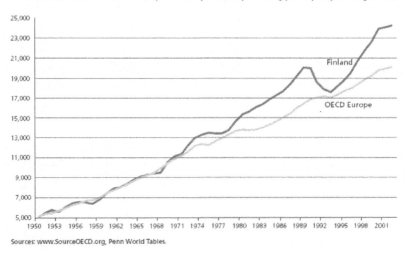

Sources: www.SourceOECD.org, Penn World Tables.

Figure 1 shows that the Finnish economy grew rapidly at that time and because of that, during the 20th century, Finnish GDP per capita grew at an annual rate of close to 3 percent, that is faster than in any other European country (The downfall in the middle of the 1990s was because of the economic crisis there which hit Finland at its hardest. But I will later explain those developments in detail).

There was a kind of general consensus in Finland that the process of industrialization was pushed forward trough massive investment in the latter described, export oriented forestry sector. In doing so the Finnish government especially used foreign technology and know-how instead of their own since it was not developed that far. Therefore Schienstock (2004) had named Finland the "wood-society[2]". Related to those arguments the consequence can be drawn that the Finnish growth-path was mainly stamped by the forestry cluster.

A special role in the structural development process of Finland was dedicated to Russia. Over years Finland was the major trade partner of Russia. According to Schienstock (2004), Finnish trade with Russia amounted to 15%/20% of the overall

---

[2] "[...] wurde Finnland auch als Waldgesellschaft charakterisiert" (p.11)

7

Finnish export rate. At that time nearly all export sectors were deeply connected to the Soviet Union. Also at the end of the 1880s, when Finland was under Russian rule, another crucial change was initiated by the Finnish authorities. In order to circumvent the Russian telegraph regulations, the Finnish Senate gave out several licences to private companies to enable them to engage in telecommunication activities. When Finland became independent in 1917, a public telecommunication sector was established while at the same time the private sector could develop further. The structure of Finnish telecom markets established over a century ago was exceptional up until the 1990s, as it enabled interaction "between operators and equipment suppliers, unlike in other countries which had resorted to monopolies" (Paija 2001, p. 2). The origin of this exceptional market can be traced back to the Finnish Senate of 1880, which granted several private licences to engage in telecommunications activity that circumvent Russian regulations. After the independence of Finland in 1917, a state telecom operator was established to operate the army and telegraph telephone network left behind by the Russians. The Finnish tradition of "duopoly" (Paija 2001) in the telecommunications sector, which means the ongoing parallel existence of both state and private telecommunication operators, is essential for a proper analysis of Finland's current success in the field of ICT. The dual structure of the telecommunication segment, which has persisted for almost a century, has created a solid foundation for equal competition, so that when the market was completely liberalized in the beginning of the 1990s, Finland did not have to suffer from complicated regulations, which were necessary in other countries to create a somewhat equal situation for the new competitors. Competition in the field of ICT also led to the environment that entrepreneurs had to be innovative in order to stay competitive. Next to an almost obligatory price war, telecommunication operators started to engage in wireless communication. In 1991, this resulted in the world's first act of commercial wireless communication, when a call with a Nokia mobile phone was made over a Nokia wireless network in Helsinki (Paija 2001).

In addition to that the Finnish government did not miss to build up a sort of network structure which can be in my view identified as the basic "foundation pillar" of the actual existing Finnish knowledge-based economy. In the middle of the 1970s the central features for the national technology politics were already established. According to that, it began to emphasise information technology. The Finnish National Fund of Research and Development (Sitra), the Technical Research Centre (VTT) or the

Academy of Final can be identified as those features. But before I will focus my work on the development and importance of the ICT-cluster it is necessary to mention the economy crisis in the 1990s, which struck the Finnish economy at its hardest.

2.2) The Crisis of the 1990s and the "Way Out"

- *Finnish Economy under Pressure –*

Schienstock (2004) pointed out that at the beginning of the 1990s Finland had managed, because of low unemployment rates and high growth rates, to be in line with the rich Nordic (industrial) countries[3]. This "catch-up process had stopped when Finland was hit by an economic crisis. In 1994 the unemployment rate raised to 20% and the Finnish Bank was confronted with a possible bankrupt. The collapse of the Soviet Union was in my eyes the major reason for this crisis because Finland therefore lost his major trade partner. Since this crisis the Finnish government had to search for a way out of it. Therefore it can be followed that with the change from the forestry cluster to the new ICT cluster, Finland managed to escape from a possible lock-in situation because of his path-dependency. Concerning the crisis, Finland was pushed forward to restructure its economy and to adjust its position in the global world market.

In line with my restructuring argument another development can be noticed during the 1990s. In the beginning of the decade, Finland experienced a heavy recession. The GDP declined by 10,4 per cent between 1990 and 1993 (see figure 2), which is for industrialized countries in peacetime highly extraordinary. Already in 1994, the GDP increased by 4 per cent again. On the other hand, the economic growth in Finland remained one of the highest in the entire EU. Jalava and Pohjola (2002) explained this sudden recovery of the Finnish economy by the important role of the production of ICT goods and services has played. In my pint of view this is true, as it will be explained in the following chapter.

---

[3] "Am Ende der 80er Jahre war es Finnland mit relativ hohen Wachstumsraten und geringer Arbeitslosigkeit gelungen, Anschluss and die reichen nordischen Industrienationen zu finden." (p.12)

Figure 2: *Annual growth rates of GDP volume, hours worked and labour productivity in Finland, 1976–1999*

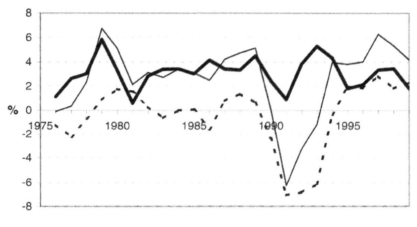

——— GDP at 1995 market prices ▪ ▪ ▪ Hours worked ▬▬▬ Labour productivity

(Source: www.finnfacts.com)

Summing it up it can be said that the phenomenon as a whole – first a very heavy recession for three years combined with an economic growth of 4 per cent subsequent to it – not only shows the relevance of ICT. It furthermore gives an impression of what an enormous industrial and commercial structural change Finland underwent in the beginning of 1990s. This change "has lead to an industrial restructuring in the former forest and metal based economy, in which knowledge has replaced capital, raw materials and energy as the dominant factor of production" (Steinbock 2004, p.11). After the recession, the economic focus shifted from raw materials, capital and energy to knowledge-intensive and expertise-oriented activities. It can be added that "from a period of slow growth and low contributions, we have moved to an era of rapid growth with opportunities for high contributions" (Rouvinen & Anttila 2003, p.9). I think that it can be emphasized as well a possible negative side of the whole new situation. Because of Finland more or less suddenly being part of the global economy, this imposes fluctuations, high risks and other new threats to the country and maybe Finland will loose in the global competition.

Finally, we can conclude from this section that both the timber and the telecommunication sector were crucial for the development of the Finnish economy.

Finland has avoided a possible lock-in situation by investing in future oriented technologies and industries, and by restructuring its whole preference in economy. As it is said above, forestry has been crucial for the Finnish economy for centuries but one has to point out that its importance declines increasingly (see Figure 3). The opposite is correct for metal and engineering industries. Although Finland began early to engage in telecommunication systems, which are a fundamental part of the named ICT sector, it

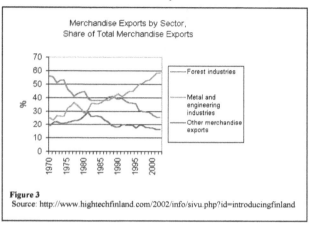

Figure 3
Source: http://www.hightechfinland.com/2002/info/sivu.php?id=introducingfinland

becomes visible that only by the end of the 1980s, beginning of the 1990s, respectively, this part of industrial production became more important than forestry. In the early 1990s, Finland's prospects seemed gloomy. In 1990, it was hit by the most severe economic crisis in any OECD. Real GDP dropped by over 10 percent in just three years, and unemployment had risen to nearly 20 percent by 1994, as I have pointed it out above. Among the factors contributing to the crisis were a downturn in the nationally vital forest-related industries, disruption in the country's sizable eastern trade due to the collapse of the Soviet Union, a speculative bubble in the domestic securities and real estate markets fueled by uncontrolled credit expansion and favorable terms of trade, and mismanaged financial liberalization, "which eventually led to credit crunch and excessive private sector indebtedness" (Rouvinen & Anttila 2003, p.13). In the latter half of the 1990s, Finland was nevertheless one of the fastest growing countries in the world. Its remarkable recovery and stellar performance are in considerable part attributable to developments in the ICT sector. This development into a knowledge-based economy with the growth of the ICT sector now will be analyzed in the next chapter of my essay.

3) The Development and Importance of the ICT cluster

- *"The New Finnish Economy"* –

Finland with only 5.2 million inhabitants has made its way from path-dependency and possible lock-in danger to become the "leader in internet connections and mobile phones per capita" (Steinbock 2003, p.27). While smallness and specialization increase a country's sensitivity to external shocks, small economies have developed various ways to cope with the problem. These include not only macroeconomic policies but also many kinds of networks and social security systems. Networking and cooperation in society in general, and in the business sector in particular, have proven to be important in developing new technologies. In many ways Finland can be characterized as a "network society" (Rouvinen & Anttila 2003). Of course, social networks, often labeled social capital, can become too tight and finally an obstacle for change and industrial transformation. Thus far, however, networking and cooperation have been an advantage rather than a disadvantage in Finnish industrial development. How this development has taken place will now be analyzed in the next chapter.

3.1) From Raw Materials to Mobile Communications

-Turning Tradition into Modernization –

As will be discussed below, most of the structural change in Finnish economy is attributable to the ICT sector. And within that sector, mobile telecommunications equipment manufacturing and especially Nokia dominate. According to Rouvinen & Anttila (2003, p.90), "in the latter half of 1990s the Finnish economy grew at an annual rate of approximately 5 percent. The contribution of Nokia to that growth was on average more than half a percentage point. In 2000 it peaked at one and a half percentage points, when the GDP growth was 6 percent", which shows to some extent the rapid change in Finnish economy. The pace and intensity of the growth process in the Finnish electro-technical industry has been extraordinary throughout the 1990s. It has lead to an industrial restructuring in the former forest and metal based economy, in which knowledge has replaced capital, raw materials and energy as the dominant factor of production. The new ICT-cluster was therefore the first major cluster in Finland in which the importance of raw materials is secondary to that of knowledge. Logically, the ICT-cluster has been the fastest growing cluster in Finland. Furthermore, Finnish

national research institutes conclude in the mid 1990s that the future rested in the ICT-cluster, which "will become one of the cornerstones of the Finnish economy, alongside the traditional industries as forest and metal behind this scenario there is the phenomenal growth of global demand [in ICT-products]" (Steinbock 2003, p.25). So it can be followed that Finland's economy of path dependency, and raw material liability is characterized by a dominating shift in policy thinking and development towards a highly specialized, knowledge based economy, which has now turned Finland to number one in national competitiveness. Before trying to explain this structural change towards a new ICT-cluster, specialized in mobile telecommunication with its flagship company, Nokia, it is first useful to explain what a "cluster" really is and what it looks like in Finland.

According to Rosenfeld a cluster is "a geographically bounded concentration of similar, related or complementary businesses, with active channels for business transactions, communications and dialogue, which share specialized infrastructure, labour markets and services, and face common opportunities and threats". Steinbock (2003, p.28) argues in a similar direction, pointing out that "a cluster is a geographically proximate group of interconnected companies and associated institutions in a particular field, linked by commonalities and complementarities". Therefore a cluster can range from a single city or state to a country or even a network of countries. Networks are a dominant factor regarding clusters. The Finnish cluster, as mentioned above, relies on the information and communications technology cluster, shortly ICT-cluster. This is a relatively broad definition which will help me to figure out the main aspects and characteristics of the actual Finnish ICT-based economy.

Figure 4:

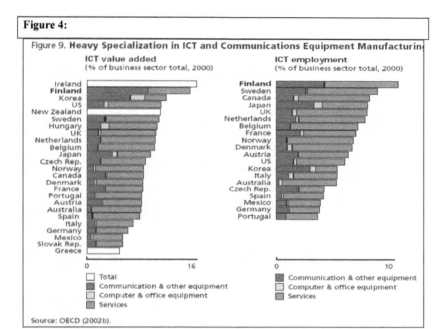

Figure 9. **Heavy Specialization in ICT and Communications Equipment Manufacturing**

ICT value added
(% of business sector total, 2000)

ICT employment
(% of business sector total, 2000)

Source: OECD (2002b).

Another thing that has to be remembered in talking about Finnish ICT-clusters is the fact that the extraordinary focus of this ICT sector on a single industry, mobile communications, has occurred alongside the equal extraordinary dominance of one single company, Nokia. But this will explained later on in more detail. In Finland, ICT companies exist in a cluster with other industries, research institutions as well as universities and polytechnics, respectively.

In the 1990s Finland became the world leader in high-tech trade surplus among indigenous high-tech producers (Paija 2001, p.3). As we can see in *Figure 4*, those arguments are stressed by OECD measurement. In my eyes, there is strong competition between the USA (Motorola) and Finland (Nokia), both struggling for the leading position in the mobile market sector. The top positions of Finland in global ICT comparisons show that it not only overtook the USA as the major ICT power, but also became the leading ICT economy in the EU. As already described above, one reason for Finland's current success in ICT is its long tradition of telecommunications and competition in that sector. The support and basics for those shift to knowledge-based and future orientated economy path was established in Finnish society along time ago.

Although Finland definitely had an advantage when telecommunication markets were liberalized, this explanation for the Finnish ICT success story does not seem sufficient. But, according to Paija (2001), in order to try to explain what is behind the success of the Finnish ICT, we cannot only exclusively focus on the ICT sector itself but have to see it as a piece of a bigger entirety. Paija says that Finnish ICT sector "must be examined within the concept of a cross-cluster concept" (2001, p.4). One reason for such a cross-cluster analysis is that the ICT sector itself seeks cooperation with other sectors. The motives behind the creation of intersect oral networks are rather simple in the first place. First of all, the ICT segment is highly aware of its fragility so that cooperation with actors from other economic spheres appears to be a rational means to spread risks (Paija 2001, p.4). If one sector's economic strength declines, there are still other sectors to rely on. There are no obvious reasons why such a polycentric strategy, which is actually more known from national economies, should not apply for single branches of industry.

Furthermore, Paija points out another important reason for cross-sectoral networks. Through cross-cluster networking the ICT sector cannot only revert to its own employees and information systems, but is enabled to exploit external expertise and information as well. This is a crucial advantage for a sector that is increasingly dependent on innovation. Cross-cluster networking creates conditions favorable to the emergence of innovations because it brings together people with completely different ages, academic background and experiences.

Maybe it is also important to emphasize here that there is of course not only one ICT cluster in Finland but several, like for example in the Helsinki metropolitan area, and cities like Tampere, Oulo or Jyväskylä. A good example for this argument is Technopolis Ventures, which was earlier called Otaniemi Science Park. This science park in Espoo, which is close to Helsinki, is Finland's biggest technology park whose focus clearly lies on information and communication technologies and was often compared with Silikon Valley in the USA. The "Finnish Wireless-Valley", as it was called by Steinbock (2003), Otaniemi is a combination of a technical university, a research centre, and a business centre and brings together 14 000 students and over 8000 professionals[4]. Here, we can see the network intense research/innovation structure in the Finnish economy. The ICT-clusters are therefore highly localized. One of the companies that has its headquarters in the park is for example Nokia, the "driving

---

[4] http://english.espoo.fi/xsl_taso1_ilmanajank.asp?path=5731;6625;7869;16404

engine" for the new Finnish knowledge-based economy because, "as Nokia is the primus motor of the Finnish cluster, the majority of the cluster firms are, at least indirectly connected to Nokia's network" (Paija 2001, p.5).

Another crucial decision of the government was to allow foreign ownership. The internationalization of the Finnish capital markets was so successful that 74 per cent of the total capitalization of the Helsinki stock market was held by foreign investors. Furthermore, the Finnish authorities have put a focus on the promotion of mobile communication systems. The increased public R&D payments also affected universities and other research institutions. Strengthening higher education facilities was crucial in order to establish a basis for the Finnish ICT sector. With regards to the ICT cluster in the area around Helsinki the two universities and the eight polytechnics are of great importance since they have provided significant ICT training which is of course crucial for the development of an ICT oriented economy. They are part of the telecom/mobile network system, which "keeps the system running". A well established tradition of close cooperation of higher education institutions and industry already existed long before the restructuring towards ICT began. The role of the government was here to intensify these relationships which were supported by generous grants supporting collaborative projects (Steinbock 2004). Especially Nokia made use of those new government decisions and started to enlarge and upgrade its influence and dominating position.

Before looking in more detail at the importance of the "driving role" of Nokia described above, let me first analyze the Finnish stage of innovation force, which is also very important in explaining its way towards the knowledge-based economy.

3.2) The Dominance/Importance of the Mobile Telecommunication Sector

- *The Wireless Miracle –*

According to Paija (2000, p.2), "during the decade, Finland became the world leader in high-tech trade surplus (High-tech exports/imports ratio) among indigenous high-tech producers". This way to specialization has made it possible for the Finish economy to break out of its path dependency, turning new features positive outcomes.

Figure 5: *The contribution of the electro-technical industry to GDP*

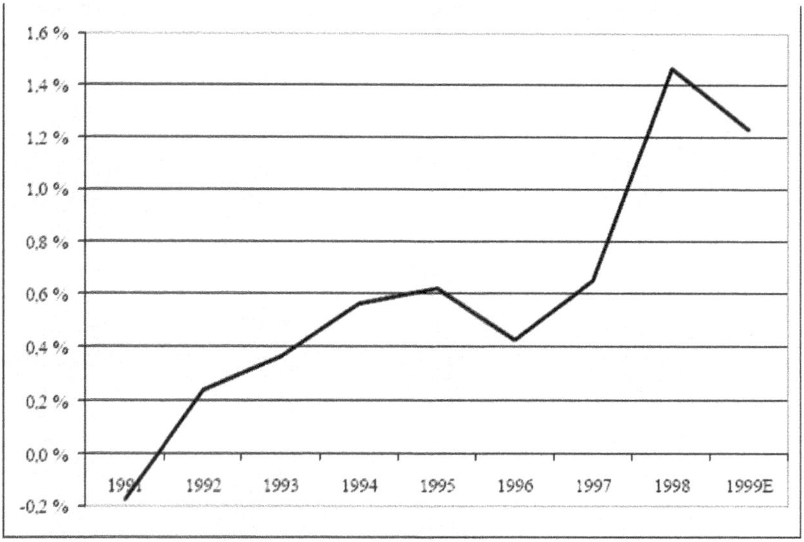

Source: Paija 2000

The share of electronics and electro-technical exports has almost tripled at the expense of pulp and paper and metals, representing close to 30 per cent of the total manufacturing exports. Behind this structural change, there is the boom in the telecommunications market in which Finland has succeeded in taking the leading position. It has a 30 per cent stake of the global mobile phone market (Paija 2001). In the wake of the boom the industry has grown at an average 20 per cent yearly growth rate, and it has become an important contributor to the GDP. In 1999, the industry contributed to the GDP growth by 1.2 percentage points (see Figure 5).

Figure 6:

Figure 2. **Explosive Growth in Electronics Since the Early 1990s:**
Finnish Manufacturing Production Volume by Industry (€ billions in 2000 prices)

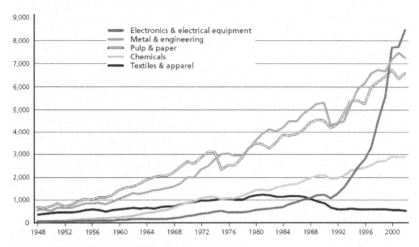

Sources: ETLA database, Hjerppe et al. (1976), National industrial statistics by *Statistics Finland.*

In addition to that, Figure 6 shows the exploded importance of the telecom-sector including mobile telecommunication in Finland. Catching a leading position in the world economy was only possible because Finland had become aware of the necessity to specialize in one field to optimize the outcomes. This shift in policy thinking had concentrated Finnish power of economy on the ICT-sector, which therefore is based on mobile phone production and supply. According to Paija (2000), in 1998, the value of ICT export products was around EUR 7 billion which was almost 20 per cent of the total export value, while in 1990 the share was only five per cent. Therefore Finland has become the most specialized OECD country in the telecommunications equipment exports. It has surpassed Japan and Sweden in the export specialization during the 1990s. And within the ICT-sector, as I have pointed out before, mobile telecommunications equipment manufacturing and Nokia dominate. "In the latter half of 1990s the Finnish economy grew at an annual rate of approximately 5 percent. The contribution of Nokia to that growth was on average more than half a percentage point" (Rouvinen & Attila 2003, p.91). From the outset, Finnish telecommunications equipment markets were open to foreign suppliers. Thanks to its small multi-operator market, Finland became a test market for the latest technology. Private operators' interest in state-of-the-art technology was fueled by the threat of being taken over by the

PTO in case of underperformance. In order to integrate different manufacturers' network equipment, operators had to develop technological expertise, which was later exploited by the emerging domestic equipment industry. The Finnish government therefore made use of this advantage and adjusted its economy to the changed demand. This was one important step towards the future oriented knowledge-based economy featuring the ICT-sector. The mobile telecommunication industry, lead by Nokia of course, made use of those adjusted circumstances and established networks and cooperation within its highly localized clusters. Finland has made its way in relying on is new strengths and powerful, market-oriented firms and enterprises. Within this ICT-cluster we can identify Nokia as the "engine" for Finnish economy and path change into the knowledge-based economy.

A central aspect in this development in the mobile telecommunications sector was the emergence of the so called Global Systems for Mobile Telecommunications (GSM), a common standard for digital mobile telephony. GSM matched to objective to of the European Commission to provide comprehensive pan-European services and standards, and to transform European telecommunications from domestic monopolies into a fully competitive environment. "Radiolinja" (The Finnet Group) sought a license in Finland to operate a second GSM network, without a competitive tendering process and finally in 1990, the provision of mobile telecommunications services was opened to competition and Radiolinja received digital GSM licenses. Because of that, Finnish mobile telecommunications operators became in 1992 the first operators in the world to offer commercial GSM service. Amidst competition, price wars, complains and intrigues growth was initially slow bit took off in 1994. Two years later, GSN accounted for 60% of all cellular users and 97% of new subscriptions (Steinbock 2004). Therefore it provided in my point of view the foundation for the growth of the Finnish telecom/mobile cluster and especially Nokia´s success.

Therefore it will be interesting, after having explained the importance of the mobile telecommunications sector for the growth and structural change of Finnish economy, to see how important Nokia is in the Finnish development process. That is what I am going to analyze in the next part of my work.

3.3) The Central Importance of NOKIA
- *"The Wireless Giant in Control of Finnish Economy?"-*

As I have already pointed out in percent sections, Nokia can be identified as the "driving engine" of Finnish economy. Especially the region around Helsinki is of great importance for the domestic ICT sector. The ICT network in Espoo is highly influenced by its biggest component, Nokia. Since it is hardly surprising that a global player dominates a Finnish ICT cluster it is of even greater relevance to point out the dimensions of Nokia's significance for the Finnish economy as a whole. Even though it has to be said that the Finnish ICT cluster comprises of a number of successful global companies, the role of Nokia as the primus motor is incontestable. It has "functioned as an engine for a whole emerging cluster" (Paija 2000, p.5). There were approximately 76 000 employees in the ICT-cluster in Finland, of which around 30 per cent (21 000 persons) worked in Nokia's Finnish subsidiaries. With a nearly 40 percent market share, Nokia is currently a clear market leader in mobile handsets, and is one of the dominant players in mobile network infrastructure equipment. "It has been riding the wave of exploding global mobile telecommunication markets, fueled by worldwide deregulation in telecommunications. Thanks to its narrowly defined and globally orientated strategy, it has been able to meet the market challenge somewhat better than its closest competitors" (Rouvinen & Anttila 2003, p. 96). Furthermore, the management has been able to build an innovation-driven culture and supporting organizational structure, flexibly exploiting both internal and external networking so Nokia had become the single most specialized one in mobile telecommunications. The broadly understood Finnish ICT cluster, from digital content provision and packing via network infrastructure equipment manufacturing and operation to end-user terminals and portals is comprised of 6,000 firms (Steinbock 2004), including 300 first-tier subcontractors of Nokia. Therefore it can be followed that the Finnish economy is highly dependent on Nokia and its success in the world market. The share of Nokia on total Finnish export is 25 percent, a number that has grown steadily since the early 1990s. Nokia´s share of the total Finnish GDP is about four per cent and such a significance of one single enterprise for a national economy is in my eyes unique.

Figure 7:

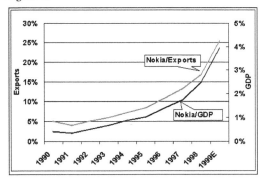

Source: http://odin.dep.no/krd/norsk/tema/distrikts/ 016061-990018/dok-nn.html#hov1

From these statistics it becomes clear that one of the impacts of Nokia on the Finnish economy is its contribution to economic growth. The company's contribution to GDP growth was approximately 1,5 per cent points per annum in the last years[5]. Next to the share in national growth, Nokia contributed a lot to the growth of the Finnish ICT sector in particular. First of all, in 1999 about half of all people employed in the ICT sector (76000) worked for Nokia (about 21000) or its subcontractors (about 15000), as it was pointed out above already, which is about one per cent of the total employment in Finland[6].

Another interesting aspect in analyzing Nokia's importance for the structural change is its share in research and development (R&D) spending which amounts to approximately 20 per cent. Furthermore, Nokia accounts for around 70% of the total capitalization of the Helsinki stock exchange (Steinbock 2004). Nokia is a typical network company which outsources the majority of the production process and concentrates on its key competence areas, namely product design, R&D and brand management. One of its key strategies is to engage actively in R&D co-operation with technology firms to induce innovation and to stay in the technological lead. It has many strategic R&D partnerships, both with small innovative enterprises and leading international ICT companies (Paija 2000).

According to Rouvinen & Anttila (2003, p.99), "Nokia has engaged the majority of the Finnish electronics industry – directly or indirectly - in the production process, and it is constantly looking for suitable new candidates to be attached to its network. The number of first-tier subcontractors is estimated to total some 300 companies. It is

---

[5] http://www.finnfacts.com/english/country/story/worldeconomy/nokia.html
[6] http://www.finnfacts.com/english/country/story/worldeconomy/nokia.html

21

estimated that the effect of Nokia on the employment of these firms is some 14 000 employees". As the production network consists of several tiers, Nokia has important spill-over effects in the cluster. In focusing on the telecommunications business Nokia has disengaged itself from some fifteen firms. Most of them have developed successfully, and today, half of them are under foreign ownership (Steinbock 2004). In other words, Nokia has given birth to number of firms which have obtained an important role in the cluster. On the other hand, Nokia has acquired, mainly abroad, recently established small firms operating in its present strategic areas to absorb and induce future technology. Therefore here we can identify another characteristic of its dominating position in Finnish economy.

The company's share in R&D (Research & Development) spending cited above already gives an idea of Nokia's importance for the whole technological development of the country's ICT sector and related businesses. Although Nokia also supports R&D in other countries, approximately 60 per cent of its R&D expenditures stay in Finland. The reason for this high R&D spending inside Finland becomes more obvious when we remember the ICT cluster in Espoo described a few pages above. Nokia is part of big high-performance network. Part of the company's strategy is outsourcing of certain parts of its business which contributed strongly to the development of ICT activity in the Greater Helsinki Region which provides the base for almost all Nokia suppliers. Steinbock (2004) therefore called the region "the Finnish Wireless-Valley" to strengthen its dependency on the telecom/mobile sector. Outsourcing has led to enormous growth opportunities and challenges for other Finnish firms, not only, but mainly in the ICT sector. R&D spending is important for Nokia itself: If the company did not invest in future human capital or technologies, it would minimize its own growth and innovation capacities and maybe will loose its leading market position.

When we talk about future human capital and R&D spending, it becomes understandable how important the cooperation between Nokia and the universities in Finland is for both sides. Especially, the cooperation with the Helsinki University of Technology, which is also part of the ICT cluster in Espoo, is important for Nokia (Steinbock 2004). The close proximity of the university to the company's headquarters and the many R&D projects implemented together give evidence about the close cooperation within the cluster. These networks are again indicators to identify Finland's way into a knowledge-based economy. For a global player like Nokia it is of crucial importance to take care of skilled future employees and the tight cooperation

with universities and research centres enables them to do exactly this. In some cases, what is good for Nokia is also good for whole Finland.

In general it can be followed that the Finnish are lucky to have Nokia in their country. The company is a major impulse for the whole economy and contributes a lot to its growth and exports. Through its strategy of outsourcing, it creates jobs and possibilities for smaller companies. On the other hand we can also think about a negative aspect of Nokia´s dominance. Of course, Nokia creates possibilities for other firms. Nevertheless, Steinbock (2004) points out that because of the company's size and importance as a customer of its subcontractors, it leaves hardly any room for developments that are not in a direct relation to Nokia and therefore leaves the smaller companies with very little "strategic flexibility".

But not only companies are completely dependent on Nokia. The whole Finnish state relies on the company's economic success because that means economic growth for the country. This dependency is in my point of view highly dangerous. Finland has hardly managed to shift its path-dependent economy of raw material to a knowledge-based and future oriented economy which on the other hand nowadays concentrates and relies too much on the success of one global player. If Nokia for example decides to move to another country for whatever reason, this would mean serious problems for the Finnish economy. As becomes clear from figure seven, one quarter of the Finnish exports is produced by Nokia. If that fell away, Finland as an export determined economy would suffer from another severe economic crisis.

Especially, the ICT sector is highly dependent on Nokia. The company's network with other ICT companies and research institutions does not only mean interconnectedness in a positive sense as pointed out above, it also reflects a great dependency of the smaller companies and research institutions on the money that comes from Nokia.

Although 90 per cent of Nokia stock was held outside Finland, it is not likely that in the coming time Nokia will (hopefully not) move to another country. According to Steinbock (2004, p.44), "Nokia's operations remain strongly concentrated in Finland" since there are no signs that point into another direction. As indicated above, the Finnish ICT cluster is not Nokia alone. Finnish subcontractors have several customers in the ICT cluster that have also expanded their outsourcing and intensified cooperation with subcontractors. For example, Sonera, the leading telecom operator is an important collaborator and demanding customer to a number of innovative internet and mobile technology developers.

On the other side some other authors like Rouvinen & Anttila (2003) or Daveri & Silva (2002) argued that there is not only Nokia. Although Finland is quite dependent on Nokia it is obvious that "the Finnish economy now has a second major pillar alongside the traditional forest-related industries" (Rouvinen & Anttila 2003, p.96). Should anything go wrong, the country has a proven ability to adapt in the past. "In addition to local OEMs, the subsidiaries of leading ICT multinationals are important strategic partners for Finnish software companies. Many multinationals (e.g. ICL, IBM, Siemens, Hewlet Packard, Ericsson, Lotus) have intensified their R&D activities and cooperation with local firms during the past years" (Paija 2000, p.6). Finnish R&D units are considered as knowledge sources or training centres from which employees are sent to other units to distribute the latest information on technological innovations, especially on wireless communication. The Finnish market is also used as a test laboratory for new innovative products and services. Although there is a possible "life without Nokia" Finnish government is highly dependent on it at the moment and tries to enlarge this position in the future.

Conclusion

The Finnish response to the most recent crisis was to open up the economy, modernize social structures, strengthen public finance, and shift policies from direct business involvement to building framework conditions for private business. The rapid turnaround of the Finnish economy would not have been possible without the rise of the ICT cluster, which in turn was facilitated by the convergence of a number of factors. As we have seen, Finland has been highly successful to carry out a structural change from forestry to ICT industries. The Finnish Miracle has brought this small Nordic country on top of the world in mobile telecommunications. Also the reaction of the government to the severe recession has been exemplary. On the other hand, Finland stays a very unique case. As I have pointed out, the basis for today's success in telecommunication has been constructed very early.

Another exceptional detail of the Finnish ICT success is the existence of Nokia. Of course, there can be endless discussions about how the ICT sector would have developed if Nokia did not exist, but it is for sure that it cannot be a best-practice for a country to be dependent on the success of one company, for the reasons pointed out above. The interdependence and networking had positive aspects for the whole Finnish economy and society. What I have tried to point out in my essay is capability and competitiveness of the new Finnish economy to adjust beneficial circumstances to create a new economy and to turn the old, path-depended economy into a knowledge-based economy with future oriented perspectives. Finland has avoided a lock-in situation and a possible collapse of its whole economy. Although the conditions were quite good, Finland was able to figure out the best practical benefits to secure its economy. Therefore I think Finland was somewhat lucky in adjusting the economy and in moving towards a knowledge based economy. One also has to consider that in line with specialisation Finland has to face some dangers. A too strong dependency on the ICT-cluster and the focusing of all institutions to benefit this cluster may limit and restrict the growing abilities of other clusters or sectors/industries. Also we can consider the dependency on Nokia as the central firm of the Finnish economy. What happens if Nokia collapses? Will Finland then be able to "keep its economy running"?

Literature

- Daveri, Francesco; Silva, Olmo, "Not only Nokia", 2002, Writing Papers Vol. 222.

- Hospers, G.-J. (2003), Beyond the Blue Banana?, in: Intereconomics March/April 2003, pages 76-85.

- Paija, L. (2000), Industrial network relationships in the Finnish ICT cluster, in: The OECD cluster focus group workshop "Do clusters matter in innovation policy" 2000.

- Paija, L. (2001), What is behind the Finnish ICT miracle?, published by The Research Institute of the Finnish Economy (Etla).

- Rouvinnen, Petri; Ylä-Anttila, Pekka, "Little Finland's Transformation to a Wireless Gigant, 2003, Etla, p.87-108.

- Schienstock, Gerd, "Finnland auf dem Weg zur Wissensökonomie. Von Pfad-Abhängigkeit zu Pfadentwicklung", RISS, 2004.

- Steinbock, Dan, „What next? Finnish ICT-clusters and Globalization", 2004, Essay Writing Papers.

Internet sources:

- http://english.espoo.fi/xsl_taso1_ilmanajank.asp?path=5731:6625:7869:16404 (accessed on 13.12.05)

- http://hdr.undp.org/reports/global/2001/en/pdf/techindex.pdf (accessed on 12.12.05)

- http://www.cfses.com/documents/workshop/houghton_1/sld004.htm (accessed on 16.12.2005)

- http://www.country-studies.com/finland/social-and-economic-developments.html (accessed on 01.01.2006)

- http://www.eduskunta.fi/efakta/vk/tuv/reginnoabst.pdf (accessed on 16.12.2005)

- http://www.elcot.com/mait-reports/finland%20ICT.pdf (accessed on 16.12.05)

- www.finnfacts.com (accessed on 14.12.05)